My Day at the
FARM

Jory Randall

PowerKiDS
press

New York

Published in 2010 by The Rosen Publishing Group, Inc.
29 East 21st Street, New York, NY 10010

First Edition

Editor: Joanne Randolph
Book Design: Julio Gil
Photo Researcher: Jessica Gerweck

Photo Credits: Cover altrendo images/Getty Images; p. 5 © Peter Beck/Corbis; p. 7 altrendo images/ Getty Images; pp. 9, 24 (top left) Randy Miller/Getty Images; p. 11 © www.iStockphoto.com/Eric Hood; pp. 13, 24 (bottom right) © www.iStockphoto.com/Naomi Bassitt; p. 15 Andy Sacks/Getty Images; p. 17 Rick Lew/Getty Images; p. 19 © www.iStockphoto.com/Jaqueline Southby; pp. 21, 24 (top right) © Hein van de Heuvel/zefa/Corbis; p. 23 © Ariel Skelley/Corbis.

Library of Congress Cataloging-in-Publication Data

Randall, Jory.
  My day at the farm / Jory Randall. — 1st ed.
      p. cm. — (A kid's life)
  Includes index.
  ISBN 978-1-4042-8077-9 (library binding) — ISBN 978-1-4358-2473-7 (pbk.) —
ISBN 978-1-4358-2474-4 (6-pack)
  1. Farms—Juvenile literature. 2. Domestic animals—Juvenile literature. I. Title.
  S519.R25 2010
  630—dc22

                                     2008050772

Manufactured in the United States of America

Contents

Today I am at the farm. The farmer tells me all about how the farm works.

I help feed the cows at the farm. They eat grass, hay, and other food.

Baby cows drink milk. When I was at the farm, I gave a baby cow a **bottle**.

Horses can live on a farm, too. Horses sometimes help the farmer do his work.

I liked petting the sheep at the farm. The sheep's **wool** is used to make yarn.

The farmer let me hold a baby pig. I loved its soft skin and its **round** nose!

I helped pick vegetables at the farm. Farmers grow lots of different plants.

I visited a farm that had sunflowers on it. The sunflowers were as tall as I was!

We went to a farm called an apple **orchard**. We picked as many apples as we could hold.

There are lots of farms that grow food or raise animals. Can you tell what kind of farm I visited today?

Words to Know

bottle

orchard

round

wool

Index

Web Sites

Due to the changing nature of Internet links, PowerKids Press has developed an online list of Web sites related to the subject of this book. This site is updated regularly. Please use this link to access the list:
www.powerkidslinks.com/kidlife/farm/

mL

12/09